Elegies for the Water

OTHER BOOKS BY PHILIP LEE WILLIAMS

NOVELS
The Heart of a Distant Forest
All the Western Stars
Slow Dance in Autumn
The Song of Daniel
Perfect Timing
Final Heat
Blue Crystal
The True and Authentic History of Jenny Dorset
A Distant Flame

NON-FICTION
The Silent Stars Go By
Crossing Wildcat Ridge
In the Morning: Reflections from First Light

Elegies

for the Water

POEMS

by Philip Lee Williams

MERCER
UNIVERSITY
PRESS

MUP/H757

© 2009 Philip Lee Williams

Mercer University Press
1400 Coleman Avenue
Macon, Georgia 31207
All rights reserved

First Edition.

Book design by Burt & Burt Studio
Illustrations by Sasha Martynchuk/iStockphoto

Books published by Mercer University Press are printed
on acid free paper that meets the requirements
of American National Standard for Information Sciences—
Permanence of Paper for Printed Library Materials.

Mercer University Press is a member of Green Press initiative
(greenpressinitiative.org), a nonprofit organization working to help publishers
and printers increase their use of recycled paper and decrease their use of fiber
derived from endangered forests. This book is printed on recycled paper.

Library of Congress Cataloging-in-Publication Data

Williams, Philip Lee.
Elegies for the water: poems / by Philip Lee Williams. —1st ed.
p. cm.
ISBN-13: 978-0-88146-142-8 (alk. paper)
ISBN-10: 0-88146-142-3 (alk. paper)
I. Title.
PS3573.I45535E44 2008
811'.54—dc22

2008042237

For Laura Jane

Endowed by
TOM WATSON BROWN
and
THE WATSON-BROWN FOUNDATION, INC.

ACKNOWLEDGMENTS

Poems here (or versions of them) have appeared in the following magazines: "Cinnamon Toast," in *Poetry;* "Bones" in *Cumberland Poetry Review;* "In Memory of Raymond Andrews" in *Mountain Laurels* and reprinted in *Georgia Voices: Poetry* (University of Georgia Press); "Something New" in *Poem,* and "Early Morning, Autumn," in *Karamu.*

CONTENTS

Losing Your Way • 1

Hearing the Silence • 3

Hermit • 5

The Lark Ascending • 6

Who We Are • 7

Box Turtle in the Driveway • 9

Rediscovering the Ivory-Bill • 10

Roadside Photograph • 11

Speaking at a Retirement Home • 13

For My Wife • 14

Starting Over • 15

Bread • 16

The Wood Pile • 18

Old Fence in the Forest • 19

Sanctuary • 20

Removing It • 21

What You Can Count On • *22*

Blackberrying • *24*

Cicada Days • *25*

Cinnamon Toast • *26*

Creek Toward River • *27*

Please Use Me Up • *28*

Parable of the Heron in Ice • *29*

Adam's Disappointment • *31*

A Promise to My Family • *32*

Sketch for My Last Words • *34*

Throwing Stones in Wildcat Creek • *36*

In Memory of Raymond Andrews • *38*

Something New • *42*

A Reminder of My Animal Past • *43*

Bones • *44*

Fishing at Grayson White's • *45*

The Tides of Wildcat Creek • *46*

Album Leaf • *48*

Path on Path • 49

Pelvic Bone • 50

Quiet Times • 52

Forest Grammar • 53

Spring Planting • 54

The Sick Man Visits Wildcat Creek • 55

The Final Country • 56

Asking Forgiveness • 57

Mourning Doves • 58

Coming Down from Black Rock Mountain By My Old Hermitage, a Stranger Gives Me Rest for the Night and Sets Out Wine • 59

My Gift of the Moon • 61

Awakening • 62

Elegies for the Water • 64

Moving the Cemetery • 66

White-Tailed Deer • 68

Against Fear While Standing In My Woods in March • 69

A Month before Spring,
I Take Stock • 70

Young and Beautiful • 71

Planting Near Highway 15 • 72

Today I Was Afraid Again • 73

The Sorrow of Mirrors • 74

For the Coming of Our Days • 75

Harvesting Clothes • 76

The Tides of Light • 77

Offering Myself to the Woods • 78

Rainy Day Ants • 79

Making Hay • 80

The Ruined Farmhouse Fills
With Crows Who Go Silent as Rain Comes • 81

What We Carry • 82

Table at the Four Seasons • 83

Right Up to the Fence • 84

Love Poem • 85

Realizing Finally That
Praise Will Not Come • 86

The Great Jade Gate
Of My Estate • 87

The Actor • 88

An Injunction • 89

For the End of the Last War • 90

Painting My Bedroom with Stars • 91

Sunday Morning on the Rocks
By the Creek, I Consider the End • 92

Learning to Grow Old • 93

The Edge of the Current • 94

It Was All About Nothing • 95

Words for the City Poets • 96

Parable of the Carpenter Bee • 97

Diplomacy • 99

Cat in the Piano • *100*

Early Morning, Autumn • *101*

A Message for You • *102*

Losing Your Way

They come back to their homing land,
The cows that ate here half a silent century past.
Pastures ran from to ditch to ditch: a fenceline
Still rusts among the dark-limbed hickories. Cattle
Lean against what tore them then and bless it.

I do not know where they have been
All this time, these hot blackberry summers
As their keepers died. Men old at sixty who lay
Among their deaths wondering of winter feed,
Their wives in sepia-tinted kitchen doorways.

The cattle are lowing, but they do not eat.
They look for changes in the weather
But cannot feel the sting of rain or needle sleet.
They ask if I am the one come to take them
Off for slaughter once more. All they know

Is a preparation for boneyards and abattoirs,
And they ask if I know them by this sound. I say
I have let the fences fall apart with tannery rust,
I have heard their hoofsteps in the August night.
I am not a farmer. I am the new fool who walks

These acres with them in the barbed moonlight;
I am their phantom veterinarian, with poultices
Made of calving nights and promises I can't keep.
They forgive me and leave moths of hair
In what's left of their boundaries on my land.

➢

The distance from tree to tree is unchanging.
I say they should look for stumps if familiar shade
Has gone missing since they last roamed the slope.
There are always markers to find, even if they have
Changed, broken down, been loved beyond memory.

Hearing the Silence

No wind. I stand high above
Wildcat Creek, preparing to die.
Not that I plan to die soon,
But soon enough, anyway.
Leaves sleep in the canopy,
Poplar, sweet gum, many hickories,
And the water is just high enough
To slip silently east toward
The equally quiet Oconee River.

I have decided that living forever
Is something I could live without.
Knowing I am perishable
Is a glory I would not miss
In this world. How else could
I listen and hear nothing
And feel this peculiar joy
Rush me outward into light?

Everything is just waiting.
There will be some reason
To move, to hunt, to love,
To laugh, to cry, to dig deeper
In the soft black soil's bed.
But now, I want to be still
With what stills me.
I will leave no footprints.
Not one thing will guess
I was alive among these trees,
But soon they will know,

And they will turn toward me
And say: He knew how to keep
The secrets of our own kind.
He knew how far we must move
To rise above our own wounds
And he did not do so. He was still.
He was among us for a long time
And we could hardly hear his breath.
And I will turn to them and say:
I have been blessed with solitude.
I can slip myself into that space
Between bark and beak,
And I have learned how birds wait
For some vernal sign to lift off,
That millipedes pause in their wandering.
I can feel a new sense cloaking us
All, the sense of silence, of held breath,
Of solemn assurances and eyes.

And so I prepare to die, and I know
The long walk home is a quiet one,
And I am ready for its first step.
But for now, I am immovable,
Plain, and silent on this shoulder
Of land, and these unrung bells
Around me shimmer, and they know
The sound of my name in this place,
Though they do not say it yet, but soon.

Hermit

Moles have come, after the rain.
Their tipping mineshafts swerve
Across the yard and into the felt mat
Of pine straw. I lie, ear down,
On the grass and hear them scat.

A proper day means no analogies
To disrupt direct experience. Narrow
Faces, whiskers waiting for my breath
To go out like rain—they wonder if I
Have the slow grace of herbaceous teeth.

I hide all day. I gestate in the closet
Of my study, unbreakable with books
That insulate the walls against storms.
I listen for the arch infirmity of rain.
I understand what is always coming near.

It takes courage to walk out the door,
Hit heat or light, that wall of knowing.
I create my own darkness as I crawl,
But I listen, and I hear the branches crack,
And I know it is coming, that it is near.

I could live in those sniffing earthworks.
I would fall in love with motionlessness
And hope that all day I would learn nothing.
I could simply dig toward insect dreams.
I could lie alone, beating into bedrock.

The Lark Ascending

I feel moonwise this morning, dancing lunatic
Of lazy ways. I may be leafing, gray greenery.

I am not the solo violin. Sorry. I flute softly
For your return. Over the road in Don's meadow

A plump shape of wings turns into summer.
There's a good reason to admire the flightful,

I guess, but this day I'm proud to be earthbound,
Wormly, wayward as a possum with no plans.

I am slow enough to touch, so come up behind me
While I'm wondering if rain is near and whisper

The password, and I will let you laugh at me,
And I will not take offense and will, in truth,

Take it as a sign of your affection that you
Find me worthy of your cheering disbelief.

All these years we spend to prove that flight
Is humanly desirable, and it gets us just above

Where we stand already, unable to know one thing
We could not comprehend from ground level.

I am tired of making sense. You know? I'll fly
When I have somewhere I want to go that's better

Than where I am already, which means I may just
Lie down, right here, for the better part of our lives.

Who We Are

I touch my grandson Caleb on his small chest
And ask, *Who is this?* And he grins to answer,
Me. Centipedes have crawled upon us lately
Down the woodslope, and they hear me
Coming, thrashing wildly toward the Fifties,
Good back, ball-sneakers, trying to live out
My life in the continuous present and past.
The deer know my age to the day, lift their eyes,
Unhurried and moss-proud frontispiece elk.

Everything watches us blunder through streets,
Down rose-dusty walkways, into lanes of camping
And watercourses. Birds know the shape of strides,
The pace of robberies and constitutionals. No flight
Is left in him, they repeat; no need to fall away
From the greening limbs into fear, to forget
Shoulders for looking back. He will turn bone,
And the thin paws scratch and scatter his jaw
Hinges wide, where we can hear his silence.

Earthworms congregate for mating, gnaw the hum
Of my footsteps, ask, *Who is this who sidesteps us
In the falling sounds?* I lie upon their land and say,
Me, this is me, and they go on with their short days.
We hone the stories of our footpaths raw, pretend
That what separates us is the source of bold union
And calm breathing. But it is not so. If I could be
Him or *her* or *them* for one morning in autumn,
All history would break down. I would be master

Of the seasons, prince with cloak and garland,
Pastoral ancestor, flower basket of our genes.

➤

It's all too much. I would be the filial ghost,
Grave white-bearded impatriarch, staffless,
Bent, unsure of anything that separates me
From arthropods and owls. They would listen
All morning, all day, through the star time,
And the considered answer would be that we
Are unseparated at birth and are slow to blossom.

In the continuous present and past, a time of day
Settles itself upon this child, says: He is not gone
Beneath the rocky soil, stone-bound; he is the one
Frogs hear walking in the wake of Wildcat Creek.
His ribs held all stories he could gather in his time.
He exhaled, and the lies of his life broke in light,
Turned the fruit colors of late-day skies. He knelt
To see what floats in still water, saw an unnameable
Face adrift with false memory. A boy should be there,

This child born for quiet harvest scenes, soft corner
Of a canvas by Millet, meditations in common time.
He dreams of saying anything but *me* to this skull
Upon the flow. He wants to be the forgotten one
At supper, to be *is* or *was* as the others need him
To fit. He comes into his consolation like a scent
Of this chosen season. He holds the boy too close
For a time, then releases him to water. They go on.
Then they go on, together, apart. This is delight.

Not *he* but *I*. In time I could know apart what is
Inevitable from what is true, but I doubt it. Now,
Here in the continuous future and present shade,
I feel the valves of my heart bloom with his smile.

Box Turtle in the Driveway

This shelter moves with her. The sky has turned cantaloupe
In the evening west, paints fruiting flesh across her dome.

I want to tell my daughter one thing quite specific.
That our lives are a slow going, that when we become

Impenetrable, seasons change, do not hold their color.
I lift the wiggling tortoise by the shellac of her shell

And say, Look, this is the ancient one, whose box gleams
In my midlife light. She bears bugs into their sleeping.

My daughter, thirteen, leans to look upon the crow's-foot
Eye of her kin. She asks one specific thing of me now.

Boy, I caught them in our woods to watch them swim
The waves of air. I turned and let them feel it, liquid

As birth in the forest afternoon. I want to tell my daughter
That moving slowly, going nowhere, is also grace.

I want to tell her that this curved hull will sail away
Tonight, going nowhere in particular, then arriving.

I have hidden things from you against my own will.
Stand on my shelled back and look for the curvature

Of love, the very thing that saves us from ourselves.
Cast a small shadow. Move against time with your life.

Rediscovering the Ivory-Bill

Nothing ever dies completely.
In the soft air of the swamp he glides
Upon the black-and-white film
Of ancestry. There must be a mate
Here somewhere in the garden
Where rivers slice the black soil.

There must have been a nest
That cradled him, comfort of wings,
The mother's vast span and croak.
There must have been rotten trees
Sweet with fern root and labial fungi.
At night their songs would break down

Like caramel over the sticky limbs.
He would look at that reflection
In the slow drain and dream the image:
I am not yet quite alone. I attend night.
I droop down to sip a skipping frog.
All the others shall see me coming

From the globe of deeper forest
Where the scent of sleeping
Lifts the ark from its anchorage.
You have seen me awaken here,
And in my low sail all extinctions
Rise. You have known wings.

Roadside Photograph

She returns. Each night at the same time
As the accident, she drifts in footless strides
To this place. She leans to look at her own
Photograph pinned to the nailed-plank cross.

That moment when the tires whispered off
The earth's face comes back. She held the wheel.
All the circular shapes in these heavens arrive.
She draws that shape in the gathering dust.

Morning glories glow in pale blue bells
Up into the shape of spars. Crickets brake
Suddenly in the forest beyond. This road
Makes no mark upon the county's maps.

She wants to know the moment of letting go,
When the whinny of her whirling made the birds
Go silent. They must have watched as she danced
The steel frame across the scar of shallow ditch.

So she returns. The flowers die as she has not
Died from memory, though she will. They lie
In soft, deer-chewed mounds beneath her
High-school face. She wore blue that single day.

Owls wait: Surely this small creature must rise
Up in the night and walk. Then they will drop
Down to catch it, twist up on shouldered wings,
Settled down to feast upon its tender joints.

➤

No fire. She did not scorch and char from it.
Like a county fair's rich shake. And she
Had no time to fear before that crack and turn.
She drew wings and found the darker air.

And she returns. Lightning bugs steer
On this film of sodden air, lead her kindly
Toward the shrine. They give off no heat,
Cannot say what soon will grow in this grove.

Already new shapes creep along her friends'
Tears, and they forget her eyes and hands.
That is the beauty of it. To be remembered
Is to be misplaced, to have gone on alone.

Speaking at a Retirement Home

I have come
To the age
Where I must re-learn
All that I forget,
So that every
Fact seems remote
Yet comforting,
Like a stained glass
Window from my
Earliest memory,
With blood and death
That looks like sleep,
Something from which
We can pretend
We will awaken,
Alive and golden,
But know too well
Is the bed where
Memory ends and
Is passed on to
Someone else,
Perhaps old loves
Who have stayed
Around and do not
Feel sorrow when we
No longer
Know their names.

For My Wife

Be easy with me.
Watch the ripe bohemian geese
Trace their memories north
Like gently honking clouds.
Come home early.
Hear the cork release
A bottle's crimson fragrance.
We can be justly proud
Of this autumn weaving,
The silvery peace
Of wings as they release.
Touch my hand
With your own heart,
Laughter, similarities
Exposed. The sand
That washes in the creek
Writes in voices, a start
Toward oceans, a sea
Of solemn civilities.
Be quiet as the afternoon
Of an old man's room
As we watch the years absolve
Us. Leave time for grieving
But not so much that we
Mistake our words for tombs.
Bind up what bends apart
Our passages. Let us resolve
To stand until we dream of rest.
Let us be changed, be blessed.

Starting Over

Go where the light is poor,
Break upon the creek-banks
In liquid splendor. Know

How much it hurts to grow
Out of belief in the shanks
Of fauns, to close that door.

Go to the aroma of beech
Trees, panorama of cattail
Spindles. Kneel and genuflect

Before the Mass of peach
And plum, hum on gnat-sail,
And in strength dissect

Your sorrows with a glade
Upon the continental heart.
Go where the dark's no flood,

And evening's glance is not a blade.
Every breath's a chance to start
Again—with flowers in the blood.

Bread

1.
Benson's bread shop downtown has been gone
For years but I can still smell the rich aroma
Of yeast on the crust of air early this morning,
As if something needed to rise before we could
Take and eat it with clover butter on the porch
Of our comparative youth. You cannot share
The memory of smells as you can old photographs
Of bulldozed neighborhoods or uncles cut down
In their prime by too much bread and salt and beer.

2.
I awaken before you in those days in our Boulevard bed
And birds audition for a part in the *Pines of Rome*
Outside the window. I sit up in bed, knowing I'm behind
In Middle English, careerist idiocy, and due in hours
At my journalism job, but already the seduction of bread
Has begun. O that smell pulls me to the porch, and I
Hold my nose into the dew-lit day and even though
We are poor I know we can afford fresh bread, so
I dress and drive to the corner store to buy a loaf of it.

3.
When there is nothing else, there is bread. When birds
Run out of food in January some old woman with hands
Like shining stones will stand in the saucer of her yard
And perform the miracle of loaves for them. Birds drop
Down the scraped-clean sky. They sing her name's notes
A thousand thousand times and come to her offered table
With wings of grace. She dies and the birds come back
Anyway to praise the house and its trees and sweet grass.
When there is nothing else, there is the memory of bread.

4.
My young wife is sitting at the table with our cat
When I return with fresh bread and butter. I have felt
The loaf, and it is this morning's, and we open the bag
And let out the bakery and sigh. The catcall blue jays
Make way for gentler songs. A Carolina wren dances
In his stately sarabande along the watching sill.
Let's give him a slice of bread, I say, and my wife says
Of course. Maybe we could feed five thousand birds
This morning with one loaf. Maybe miracles will come.

5.
How far can the smell of bread travel on a clear morning?
Do the sick smell it as we do, a summons to fecundity
And generosity? Do the nostrils of the dead briefly flare
When it passes in their long night? The smell of bread
Makes us young again, my wife and me, now grandparents
And filled with the impossible promises of risen things
That we still believe anyway; the smell of bread takes away
Sin and suffering, even if you do not believe in sin,
And suffering is a television report. This is from our bread.

6.
The smell from Benson's bread shop was the fresh gift
Given each morning when we could not pay for it, scent
Against hunger. I am young again and my wife butters
Her slice and the cat sits in her lap, and the wren sideslips
Along the sunny sill while I pour coffee and consider days
To come, aromas to come, stories that have written us
Into their own plots involving small towns and starvation
And how the people in their misery saved themselves
And blessed themselves with the great mystery of bread.

The Wood Pile

I should have cleared away
The old wood pile
When winter still held.

Now that all things
Stir in the deadfall,
Even the sine-wave snakes,

I think: let it go.
Do not worry
About what is not done

One season or never.
Waiting is also an art.
Time will clear away

The old wood pile
For me. I can hear now
The grateful insect work

Begin again, the return
Of lumbering in its season,
The small sawing of small things.

Old Fence in the Forest

A scar of barbed wire runs through our woods,
Trunk to trunk, boundary for cattle half a century
Dead. Their shades slip through. On cold-front nights
The wind gives up its bovine inflections, mourning
A lost geography. I lumber along, hoof by hoof
And listen for sleet from the milk-colored clouds.

My own scars hold me back. I want to get out of here.
I want to unfold my wings down the derby backstretch
And shred the wire without a scratch. But love is a scar
I love, and grief is a scar for which I grieve each night.
We keep our strung barbs close. We stay close to home.
We praise the music of wind along our fence lines.

Sanctuary

This land owns me, warms my feet
On a summer stroll as if to check a claim.
I am serf and source of much merriment
When I present myself for inspection.
The land might say: You're not much
And you're sure not all I have. Welcome
Anyway, among the nuthatch tracks,
The amiable syllables of the wren,
That barn owl's deceptive lullaby.
Welcome where plump rattling coils
Unwind for the quick kill. Welcome
To the kingdom of bioluminescent
Foxfire and house-wide stones on whose
Roofs you may rest for my delight.

The land takes me anyway as it takes
The creek's mild tides, the witchy deadfall,
The slivers of hickory nuts idly peeled
By squirrels in a clearing sun has made.
The land says: I see sorrow for the future
In you and no shame for it. And yet
I'll take you anyway, poor relative come
Begging, upright and easy prey.
I'll clear a path so you can pretend to know
Where you are going for all the miles
Of all your days, so you will believe
You, too, are worthy of this praise.

Removing It

In good time I will shed my skin too,
The patterns of my life, varied jewels,
Imagined diamonds, lapis, and pearls.

A boy will find it near an oak-tree flue,
Print of how I was gentle and was cruel,
Strength of color and the calm of curls.

What I leave I leave each night or noon,
The time I walked right past the rising hands
Of friends or stopped to pray a stranger's pain.

The single skin we bear comes off too soon.
We move to light among the fragrant lands
And think the moss and mist are sun and grain.

In good time I will dream the day of bones
As my littered skins lie slope to slope to show
The way alone. What I leave I leave you free.

I move to light among the solemn drones.
To find my shape go slow by slow by slow.
We shed the skin, go blind again, then see.

What You Can Count On

Meet me at the creek
Where the deer trample
Down the water greens
When they come to drink.

I will be seeing how
The peripheral ecstasies
Of wind and lilting pollen
Have changed the water-rut

Cut out of hill-slope stone
For thousands of years.
Meet me near the pottery
Kiln of Woodland women

Who knelt in the oxbow
Embrasure, safe from attack
Of other nations or the men
Of their own clan, love-mad

For spring. I will not touch
You in any way you do not wish
To be touched. Meet me there.
The only sound will be singing

Shafts of hickory and beech.
The only shadow that moves
Along the paths will be mine.
I will wait for you until death.

This is the only promise
I have left to give anyone.
If you arrive, you will know
I have kept it, safe, for you.

Blackberrying

These purpled palms give me away.
I have been lost for ninety minutes
Down the road, harvesting berries
In my hat. I have not been innocent
In years. A young girl in a dollar-store
Dress stood watching me from the lane
That leads off the dirt road to her house,
And I smiled at her and showed the stains
On both my hands. See? I am a thief
But I only steal the wild sweetness
From berry vines. She was unconvinced
That I was quite that harmless. She left.
Now, I feel the guilt of unknown crimes,
And I realize that all my life I have waited
For the law to come down on me, hard,
For the one act I did not know was illegal.
The juice upon my palms admits I am not
Her savior, never died for love or humankind,
That I just stood in the late day and plucked
Berries off and threw them in my hat,
Not knowing I was being judged. See me
Differently, I want to say, the least harmful
Man in America, one who will rip his face
With a crown of blackberry thorns before
He costs a child the smile of her sanctuary.
Some vineyards sweeten nothing. Some roads
Go nowhere. Some men never know their crimes.

Cicada Days

They sing less each day
And fall dying into the grass,
Flipping to fly. If it hurts,
Who knows the tune
To give them new sleep?
I know less each year
Of my life, words to songs,
Eyes in the morning mirror
Not mine, an old man's.
Can they hear my song?
When their wings fold up,
Still diaphanous, stained-
Windows to their carapaces,
They fade in the motets
Of August. But they return
Each summer with one voice,
One suicidal racket,
One ancient path to fly.
We join in our time
As melanoma fuses cells,
And I know, even in winter,
This song the dying scream.

Cinnamon Toast

Sugared flour, powdered cinnamon:
The essential waste delights me!
All useless things should be so shot
With calories and guilt that's guilt
Only as drizzles are storms. Spring
Should slicken and unfold as fast
As the sugar melts upon the buds.
Forgiveness should be so well formed.
That blend delights as gently
As gardenias overpower. Beignet
Not quite grown, half baked as bun,
Mildly solemn without its milk.
Lord, what pointless miseries we dream.
The earth is ripe with joy at rain.
I want to deserve that gesture,
And the sweet, twisted, butter-soaked
Glory of cinnamon toast.

Creek Toward River

Let's go. We will lie in the creek today,
Cold and folded, to float east, feet-first,
To drift dreamward with arms crossed
Like sleepers in some royal valley.

You will pace me in the lily waves
As pine whiskers float down the oxbow;
Swallowtails puddle in the gritty flutter
Of sidewash, flake off as if they burned.

We were meant for deeper troughs,
Or at least we shape the song that way,
Doric columns in the fluted chute.
We move toward the point of clarity

In our thinking. But maybe that is not
The assembly point of this foxed and friable
Lewis-and-Clark map. Perhaps you will
Outdrift me toward the lace and olive sea.

Let's go. We will go beneath the arms
Of sloped and settling trees in our voyage
Out. Your breasts will swell, leak honey
In the spring turn of shore and bodies.

While I twist in one soft and silvered eddy,
You will hit the river's long swift tongue
Like a sacrificial meal. From then on, water,
All water on the earth, will dream your name.

Please Use Me Up

My desk looks lost today in thought,
And maybe its steady plane recalls
A forest in northern Minnesota
From half a century ago, long before
The rip of tooth and chain came gnawing.
My bookshelves brag of their grain.
Some days the magazine rack moans
Against its hammered tacks. Then,
The whole house begins to utter,
Like Whitman, some candled chant
Of old growth in the rain-damp Northwest.
It has this bad case of shingles now,
Porches; scampering lizards tickle it
Into shivering splints. Every wooden
Part of this house begins to gather
For the ritual accusations.

We are all, each beam and joist of us,
Used up by the world, and these, our
Nails, shims, struts, planks, alabaster
Fixtures, mean almost nothing to them.
I can live with that. I can live to know
My shoulders are the surface on which
Some half-wit poet softens up the world
So it seems to make sense and sibilance.

I awaken each day to say, Use me, use me,
Saw me into perfect shapes that fit,
And do not stop until you use me up.

Parable of the Heron in Ice

Dream: Great blue heron
Grazing in a field of ice
Like a mess of broken kite,
Crashed, awaiting my rescue.
His eyes go sleep-calm.
Goats in their belled glance
Stop to see how feathers
Came into this scented place.

I don't know where to start
Saving things. With the first
Of a species or the near-last?
I can't quite make myself
Leave the edge of the woods
To find where it comes apart,
Where wing bones lie bleached
And pointing toward the air.

The older animals all say:
You choose, and in the choice
There will be fresh meaning,
But I know I cannot step out.
I am the wrong savior for you,
Can't see how wings and hair
Fit in the fender of hedgerows.
Storms get on with it, squat

And lift their skirts above us.
Knowing what to save must be
The worst kind of gift. Then, you
Have a choice to make, to say

That one pair of moonlight eyes
Will follow each dawn and noon,
And others kneel in the shower-house
Of bright and beating blood.

So this heron who should feed
In the thin mirror of a pond
Waits for me to re-dream ice,
To reach into the stories I shape
And let it go at the water's hem.
Even then I cannot quite move
To save one thing now sure to melt,
Invisible in the pale invisible world.

Adam's Disappointment

I have invented new fauna for these woods,
Pronghorn antelopes, Thompson's gazelles,
Shoot-nibbling giraffes, marsupials minus adjectives.
In that bend of the creek is the platypus cove,
And down this green wadi you will find
Polar bears, cracking at the stones for fish.
I will trade the native flora, might as well,
So here are forty-foot ferns, palm trees,
Aspens going gold-white, gold-white
Gold-white in the glowing wind.
A tiger has scented me and purrs.

To each his own Eden, I suppose,
Steamy swinging lianas, firs fragrant as a holiday,
Cubs in ice caves listening for old paws.
I wonder if those billion insect friends
Look at me in the evening and say
I fit or I do not fit in their compound eyes.
I wonder if Adam sat in his rope hammock
Wanting not a woman but a heavy snow,
Perfect flakes that fill the stumps
With pale forgiveness; wanting the inarguable,
The unequivocal wildness of ice.

A Promise to My Family

We have all made it home
Before the storm, and the wind,
Which has moaned all day,
Dies or holds its breath, then exhales
Into the bed of coming snow.

How much, really, can we know?
The work of my life fails
To reach others, isn't the way
To hold my family's hands and mend
Them before we lie in the loam.

Wife, forgive my cedar arms.
I wished to be a strong and moving force,
A soft-shoe man in your streets,
As it were. But I prefer to hold
Here from the storm, love-bound.

Daughter, hear the springtime sound
That comes among my soft cold
Strides. My love for you heats
Up continents, though, of course,
Without their periwinkle charms.

And so. And so. I want this much
To build the fires that keep you snug
For all your lives. I want to blow away
The ice gods, the sun-struck dances
Of danger. But this is to admit I fail.

When I seem cold, know I am hot
In the core. If I do not takes the chances
Bolder men will know, I mean to say
That I lie happy in the hole I've dug.
And to you in storms? My promised touch.

Sketch for My Last Words

I do not want
My last word
To be a verb
Or adjective,
A frail shout.

Let me find
A noun upon
My lips, say
*Honey, leaf,
Light, cone.*

If a tree can
Decide the way
To fall down,
I could list
All the nouns

In which I lie:
*Bed, arms,
Sunlight, lace.*
I could sell
My adverbs

In the month
Before I die,
*Gladly, sweetly,
Madly, lovingly.*
The articles be

Damned. The
Sky will molt
Clouds, and I
Will hold out
My hand and say:

Rain,
Violets,
Earth,
You.

Throwing Stones in Wildcat Creek

A string of waves unravels from the heart
That sipped my stone. It spools east toward
The river. Air, light, seas: waves move all of them
Toward or away from me. I want my life to
Have waves, too, meaning, a victory or two
Among the cinders. I want too much to ask.

I want too much to ask of my friends and trees,
Of the wave-risen crows and wild peacock cries.
I want too much to eat, too many choices of wine.
I want to know the exact meaning of every word
Every person ever speaks in my presence, so I can
Explain the inner folds, the origami workings of
This spongiform Earth. I want too much to ask.

I want a quartz crystal that breaks light
Into the colors of my nighttime sorrows.
I want time to straighten myself out, to bring back
The young man with no gray in his beard
And who dreams of writing rooted books and thinks
How wonderful it will be. I want to be a published
Author! I want to believe I have not wasted my life

As James Wright or Ezra Pound came to believe
They had wasted theirs. I want to start over without
Any particular desire except to treat those I love
Better than they treat me, always, always, to sing
Like the most profound minnesinger to his fancy love,
To bring messages, not from the other side of death,
But from this side, the one in which we find glory.

I want to invent peace and then destroy each trace
That leads back to me. I want to be invisible and present
At the same time, so I can know what you really think
Of me, and then I can change, meaning into a wave,
But this is too much to ask, so I only beg for you
To come looking for me when I have gone away,
Even if you know you will never find me, not now,
Not ever, not in a thousand million lovely lifetimes.

In Memory of Raymond Andrews
(1934-1991)

1.
Our restless country shifts in its ice,
Old friend. A January once more holds
Me near the fires where black cats roll
Up and over for a stretch. I bless
That idleness and the letters of your name,
Sink in dreams to your cool reef,
Then rise against it. That laughter
Has me waiting, for you might come here
Once more with beer and magazines
To my front door, all shades of delight.

2.
I shook your soft hand that June
Near Madison Square Garden. You wanted
To spring for Irish coffee, but I left
You and went up in the Penta twelve floors
To bed. We might have gone back
To O'Reilly's, as we did years before,
And drunk all night. You slipped
Past me down that last sidewalk,
Rolling gait, no capacity for enduring
The brotherhood of our failures, tired
Beyond the traffic and the tearing light.

3.
I want to bless that turning away,
Its fatal separation, shake milkweed
To stir our country alchemy; thaw
The night back and go from there.
I want you to sponge that last meal
Off Margaret, have you lead the crew
From Maria's south down the sidewalk,
Ray. I want to change my mind now.
I will go with you for Irish coffee
And chart our Southern lives toward home.

4.
All that last night you wrote notes
For the disposition of your manuscripts, books,
When autumn had come gold and red
Back to Georgia. You took the weave of age,
Spread that uneven tapestry half across
Your house in the woods. You came
Past old lapses, memories of baseball,
Funny-paper stories from the Thirties
When you and Benny were only boys
In Madison. I consecrate all the layers
Of that last long evening before us.

5.
You came back South for that end.
Half of your life in the city, never stopped
To drive, arrived here broken up
And lost to us by bus that season.
I did not dream a solid darkness
Had brought you home. The fresh words
Gone, wild ache of new books faded
To your shelves. I did not dream all
The blank stares had come for you;
The quiet distance had come for you.

6.
You went to the gazebo. The pistol
Had the mass of stars. Words came.
You were sick then, tired, innocent
For your life of hurting anyone, anything.
You spoke to that clear pain. Night
Had come soft and cool, and each star
Held down that black and ending sky.
You held the pistol up and fired.
The shaken earth swayed close.

7.
And now another winter, two years after
You fell. A cold rain rests on Georgia,
Sliding from the thicker oak trunks to moss
And the red earth and a bed of leaves.
There is no resurrection of your body here
Today. Your ashes and their molecules
Spin somewhere near me, and I remain
Alive and broken, or not, as the day permits.

My daughter you never met sips milk
By the January fire and calls to me.

8.
I praise the artlessness of your life,
Ray, that spring in your step, how
As you drank everyone around you grew
Steadily more wonderful. I praise old films
And the Brooklyn Dodgers, your command
Of trivia, genuine risk of real affection.
I praise memory and age and wisdom
For my own purposes, my other life.

9.
Listen to me, Ray: my anger has gone,
But it took my breath to drive past
Your unexpected act. I want to say
I live in your memory, but all sure
Things break down to light and ashes.
I want to say your voice endures
In my hands, that I am your witness
Against this life, that in my quiet days
I hear your deep laughter outside
My front door somewhere toward morning.

Something New

My sweet land is not yet growing
With honeysuckle and shadow.
Along the creek slopes, the moss clings
To winter, damp fibers ringing
The memory of wildflowers and sun.
All winter I have felt the jonquils
Bursting from my skin, cats crazy
For warm rolling grass,
The silver flames of spring colors along my creek.
I know if one more season comes
A chance will rise for me
To brush these stray failings back,
To rush once more at love
As if it were seasonal,
The sound of wings, the color of light.

A Reminder of My Animal Past

The horse returns for my funeral.
Not yet, I tell him.
When you see me lumber,
Stagger toward water,
Wane, whirl,
I am still learning
To dance
In the long cool shadows
Of the barn. I was alive
The last time we ran
Through the hayfields,
Both of us chest-deep,
Scrubbed clean,
Close to harvest.
Don't give up on me now.

Bones

I step in line. We sway
Along in the riot of orchids,
Tropical rot of intoxicants,
And we are halfway there
Before I know we seek
The elephants' burial ground.
I lumber with them,
Old legs heavy with peace.
I feel the next one's breath
Prod me along past waterfalls
Jeweled in the late day's light.
I believe I hear singing.
All my wordless days
I have wanted to believe
I could sway among their tusks
Toward home, with paws above us
Trailing petals and praising
How each day is an act of birth,
And each enduring night
The ancient path toward bones.

Fishing at Grayson White's

I cast the line far out, away from reel
And hand, the configurations of delight
Apparent in musculature, the whispering
Horizon, one small splash out there.
I grieve for water. Clouds spread east
Across the surface, green and patient
For a breeze. Bream come up toward me.
I lay across the delicacies of that surface
And drift out into the lake with birds
Low and skimming small familiar ripples.
I could sink toward hydrilla and childhood.
I could spread my fins like wet sails,
Get caught by eddies, pushed on south
Toward the dam. I could exhale geese.
At the end of discovery is the fair beginning
Of another cast. I make that old motion
With its splendid spell, its dying arch.
I find that I am caught on this edge
Of sand and water, taut against the lines.
I find consolation. I rise to the bait.

The Tides of Wildcat Creek

I am frozen at the edges today.
The course of my creek escapes me,
Going for the river across posted land.
I have lost the map of my veins
And capillaries; the stuck mitral valve
Of our well-pump is a mystery.

Some days the trail just grows cold.
Beech trees shed their carved lovers'
Initials; I pass the dark landmarks
Of childhood and miss the turn-off
From innocence all over again. Water
Is the track of ice. I flow along.

We sandbagged it last summer, saw
A pool rise three feet reflecting green.
Storms melted the sand away, changed
The course. My own movement turned
In the moon toward adolescence, calm
Soft chime of the milkweed and wheat.

Gail Fambrough, I remember you.
An appendectomy killed you in my
Second grade class. They lay your
Face among that straight hay hair
And closed the rank of desks up one.
I draw the contours of that lost smile

And do not grieve. You flow on
In my secondary heart. I mention
Your frayed coatsleeve to bring back
The smell of creosote and sandwiches,
Shape of old tree roots for a throne.
A knot of rock choked me off.

I stare at Wildcat Creek to turn it
South away from the Oconee River.
No luck. My ice-bound hands hold
A fragrance of mild regret. I am sung
By the fading path. I am forever found
At the far end of that trail.

Album Leaf

The moon is at issue in our house tonight,
That herald of gravitational pull
And soliloquies. I lie awake next to you.
For days I have wished to make a speech,
To break aloe and drip it over your palms
With words of impeccable sincerity.
Your breath beside me in our bed
Is my sinecure. My space is tenuous
Next to you, a man without Victorian
Guarantees. There are no reserved rights.
I cast upon that steady breath
Moonlight petals, old sanctimonies.
After coffee in the morning I will
Tell you weather, all the subtle signs
Of pressure building in the Plains.
You will know the wounds I really mean:
We heal what is not broken,
We bind what cannot break.

Path on Path

I made these paths toward water,
Switchbacks down the shouldered leaves.
What arrives upon my land can never go
Away from all this quiet again.

Every living and unliving thing here
Has a soul or something like one,
It seems to me. Call it memory or structure,
Or the glint of sun upon the shingled moss.

I could spend each fractured day writing
Obituaries of leaf and bark, owl-notes,
Paw, creek-wash. I cannot grant a resurrection.
They break down into the sweet rot

Of memory. These paths bear my footsteps.
A daughter wears my chocolate eyes.
Perhaps the soul is memory's weathervane
Or is friable or is hard, bright as chalcedony.

Nuthatch, chickadee, red-breasted woodpecker:
These are the punctuation marks of air,
And in those blue sentences, somewhere rising,
Is the story of my own intention to believe.

If there must be souls, let them be built
Path on path, like a map of all intentions
In a single lifetime; let them point the way
South when we sense the newly sharpened chill.

Pelvic Bone

1.
Dogs killed it, probably. The eyes wide
With knowledge. The first spring smells
Settling, guided to the loamy richness
Where the beech trees begin toward water.
Later, in the deep hoof-beats of retreat,
Its mother would recall the soft brown
Hair. She would not care when that baying
Came once more. You can lose so much
That memorial bones mark not one thing,
Not passage, not the squeak of suckling,
Not the warm huddled heart of March.

I hold it to the light this aging afternoon,
Admit my vast complicity. I feel the marks
Of teeth mad for marrow on the saddle
Of its last standing. My own flesh is torn
From the companion bone, borne away.

2.
We cannot know if we are chosen,
And that is the single sign among the oaks
Of my forest. We have been sighted,
Must await that coming. We ride the pelvis,
Hard white horse, into a safer place,
We think, to find claws and teeth there
For us, patient, knowing we will kneel.
I will not betray my kind by giving death
A name of his own. I deny him three times
Before the sun rises through the pine blades.
We shelter secrets from the young.

And yet they know it well enough,
That some do not return from the far glen
For bedding down beneath the warm heart
Of wind. They know that every lie we tell
Is sweet grass. That is how love starts.

Quiet Times

Quiet times do not
Necessarily mean peace.
The deer, turned stone,
When it hears my feet.

Quiet times may hear
What the speaking world
Will miss to shout out
The latest shame or score.

Quiet times may not
Know more than gears
That gape and grind at mills.
But my own damp fears

Suggest the opposite may
Be true, that quiet times
Can shingle over rotted roofs
So expertly that a barn owl

Would glance down, see moss,
Hear nothing but the leak
Of women's daily loss,
The tears to swell my creek.

Forest Grammar

My woods fill with the winter punctuation of deadfall.
I step up to a hickory comma and pause. Cold words
Whisper themselves into sentences around me,
And I ask my migratory translators for more time.

A sunstroke lingers in a mound of deer periods.
New paragraphs shake themselves loose from oak trunks.
All the cold green winter annuals live lower case,
Parenthetical (to a fault), never rousing once to exclaim.

The new season's red pen unlimbers itself, ready to mark
Each semicolon pebble. I begin to know the hawk acrostics,
The cool green dash of moss grown spongy with rain.
I hear the wind shape its night lips for vowels.

A question-mark oak holds down the pasture, now green,
At the end of our road. Soon, when leaves surprise it,
We will forget its interrogatory shape. But now, bareback
In the long slow slope, we read it right, by the rules.

My woods keep their place with the sun's old angles.
Each day they know where they left off the story,
Where to begin in the syntax of sumac, how to tell
Who I am, where I am going, and when I will get there.

All my life I have awakened in the stubborn syllabary
Of changing seasons and found myself weeks behind.
I drive my grammar into each step. I am the other
Apostrophe, the one that encloses these, our lives.

Spring Planting

I take the grass seed in my palm.
Each memorial chute makes choices
It can't promise. So do I, such as watering
Each day, a proper amount only or at all.
We go at it solemnly, vows that we begin
To break as I fling them into shallow tine lines.
Promises are unnatural, meant to be made
With gifts of rich earth and fertilizer,
And sun starts cheating right away, baking,
Raining, ruining all pledges, withering
Whatever sprouts. We should be better
To each other than this. You should grow
In all weather and I should stand guard
By moon and stars against frosts and mud,
With straw to save you from washing away.
Then you could watch me grow each day,
Amazed at how in this world each story
Can begin at any point of possible germination,
Near the beginning or just before the end.

The Sick Man Visits Wildcat Creek

I took my migraine aura to our creek this morning
And cast it on the moving waters. I could not tell
Which light was mine
And which shine spangled off the coming spring.
The stream glowed gold with coins of my disease
Or the coming of a shimmering season—
I did not mind that I would never know.
We do not need the truth to sing.
We do not need to rise to know the rose.

The Final Country

Old men know the limits of small countries.
Each nation's boundary lies from stone to stone
In the green pasture's slope. Each land has a name,
And it is an old man's last name that builds
A boundary. We travel there, dreaming they rise
From street to street in their capital towns.

I want to stop defending what I cannot own.
I want to lie, still living, among them, in their towns,
And put my ear to the soft warm earth
And hear them whisper *soon enough, soon enough.*
In sleeping robes, you will be a ruler soon enough.

Asking Forgiveness

Over night
A luminous place
Has settled in my name,
As if to say I do not need
More of this world
Than I have already,
As if my name
Had been gently rubbed
From the slate of ambition
And the only thing left
Is a solemn vow
To grow green
In the memory
Of my loved ones
And come back in spring
Each year like a promise
And from that far country
Bring all the love
That I have harvested
And run it like a warm bath
On those who suffered for me.

Mourning Doves

Mourning doves bathe in the spring air,
Splashing through the suds of low clouds
In their pairs of glove-gray cooing peace.

They do not mourn. We who mate for life
Know loss and know it will come for us
Like swords of lightning in a nimbus sheath.

The sound among those clouds is our answer
From the swimming mate in that gloried air
Who asks *Who?* To hear the answer *You.*

Coming Down from Black Rock Mountain By My Old Hermitage, a Stranger Gives Me Rest for the Night and Sets Out Wine

Crickets string themselves up the slope
Like small-town Christmas decorations.
They tell me the temperature. The air's ripe
For mating.

Some days I am unable to cope
With the sobriety of afternoon nations,
With the last smoke from the last pipe.
We're dating

The monuments of the Cherokee girls,
The ones who slapped and stamped the pots.
They turned to see the land once more
When they were going.

Sometimes memory unwinds and whirls
Like storm-split vines. The old home rots
And sags, and out beside the fragrant door
Someone's sowing

Flower seeds. But they must be annuals
For the Indian summer color wheel.
I lie upon the porch and sip the stars.
I'm falling

From what I knew, and all the manuals
Have been tossed or burned, my last meal
Served. I will not go back to my wars.
They're calling,

But I will not go back to my wars.

My Gift of the Moon

The moon is inexpensive tonight,
Cracked cockle shell, a porcelain chip,
Unaddressed by lovers or ancient poets
With wars or unspeakable grievances.
When no one is looking, I take it
For myself and hold it in my cupped hands
And see the bright craters of this life.

It is not time for planting yet or harvest,
Not time for the old ones to rise into chalklight
With their regrets and unsteady galaxies.
It is not time for the gibbous or the full.
And yet I hold the creamy slice with such delight
That quiet creatures come to me, step on step,
To ask if I am savior of their long-lost daytime.

I am not. I was only shopping evening stars
For my daughter when I saw the potsherd moon
Above my neighbor's hayfield, took it down
To light my sacrificial palms. To love most
We must earn least. And so this marked-down
Moon was mine for the taking. And now it's
Back in the paste of zircon stars, free and freely

Given, taken, shaped for love on this cold night.

Awakening

1.
The old preachers say on resurrection day
The graves will open and the dead will stand amazed
In that awakening light, wobbly as colts, big-eyed
With fearlessness and wonder. But I do not want
To rise unless the animals do, all the soft birds
In their shrouds of sharp red or Pacific blue,
The trout with iridescent cloaks of pale speckling.

2.
They will push up through the forest leaves
Like mushrooms, flanks hot for light.
One will test its eight arching legs; a second
Warms his fur and yawns, in no hurry to move.
In the shallows tadpoles realize this empty sleep
Means only that spring is near. Who could believe
Such a story? They do not tell it, do not care.

3.
There is no rapture without mockingbirds.
We cannot join that monkish candlelight line
Without the soft idling sound of trailing cats.
If deer do not sit up in the hidden hayfields
And look around brownly, we shall stay sleeping.
If the great whales do not sing, do not call us
To that reward. Awaken every sleeping paw.

4.
If the animals cannot come, I will stay behind
And wait for them. We will bring all paradise
With us when we come. Quill creatures, scales,
Flesh, fur, clean white bone—all will join me
To leave or stay. I am their own kind. In the drift
Of dandelions on a perfect day we will arise to learn
Each other's language. We will walk the quiet land.

5.
Always, we are choosing what to leave behind.
Old friends, family, a photographed neighborhood
Long gone to anything but memory and words alone.
So on resurrection day don't awaken to a new place
And the penitent dead but to that most perfect day
Of your life, to feathers in their strong ascent,
To the hands you held, the fur against your cheek.

6.
I want to rise with claws and keen eyes.
I want to rise with slip-scales and old tides.
I want to rise surprised by flight, taking off
From a quilted field for soft blue skies.
I want to rise in the company of animals
Who do not hate all other animals.
I want to stay behind and welcome our kind.

Elegies for the Water

Those who choose to have their ashes cast
Upon the water must choose a place to float or flow,
A stream free of pooling rocks and deadfall
Or an ocean whose warm currents drift along
The continents in search of time's new world.

They must know if they wish to drift curled
Against an owl-hunted bank of fern and song
Or if they need to hear the deeper waters' call.
They must have a sense of where all senses go,
Into one future or backward into a single past.

I wish I could cast my own ashes in the wind
And navigate the streams from air to sea in storms
And days of utter settled calm. I wish my friends
Could watch me spin into the deep idea of water
And yet have my destination plotted and planned.

We want to know, and not know, if we can stand
Where that flow takes us in the end. Are we fodder
For a simple malignancy of beginnings and ends
Or can we shift to shape ourselves in other forms
That say more of who we were until the silent bend?

I do not know if I was born for that leaving flow.
Others see it clear and plain, the pond in which
Their ashes should be cast, the stream to take them
East as heroes seeking wisdom go. Some may need
To lie in North Atlantic storms. Let them write it so.

Any water is all water, as this earth that I claim to know
In my own woods is filled from trunk to trunk with seed
That doesn't need a sprinkler or a hoe. Ash will not dim
With distance as it swims away from poor and rich.
In water, it just knows: no boat, no oars, no need to row.

Moving the Cemetery

They must be dreaming.
Sky-spread cranes, kneeling backhoes,
A scratching on the roof. What now?
Awakening from their final rest,
To hear a midnight phone ringing
And the worst news of their lives?
They had supposed the slow love
Of root and stone permanent,
But knuckles scrape, knees go
Contrapposto, and soon one eye
Opens: Is this some kind of joke?

Rain on the upfolded umbrella
Must sound like showers
On the sepulcher's roof, pattering,
Irresolute, yet so unexpected.
Diamonds of light might seep
Along the coffin seams as the box
Rises in the machinery roar.
They must be dreaming.

What now? Some subdivision,
Some hydroelectric project nearing
Completion, the church jacked up
On a flatbed moving truck?
Winter, fall, summer, spring,
Or that seasonless time between them
When neither gray nor green
Predominates, perhaps, no time at all.

And if the dead do dream,
Do they see signs in weather or earth
Or shifts in the tucked-tight landscape?
The foreman scratches his arm,
Spits, looks in the excavation
Sees a clean dig, lights a cigar.
He must be dreaming.

The dead are harvested, shucked.
They hear traffic, remember
How the migrating birds flew over
In season, shaped for flight,
Apparently motionless, thinking:
They do not know where they go.
And so they must be dreaming
Their way north or south
Or toward or away from danger
Or love or failure or their own bodies.

That could be snow. Could be petals
From the gardenia bush
That grew so close to the door
You could smell it in bloom time.

The brakes are cringing, screaming.
They must be dreaming.

White-Tailed Deer

The fawn turns statuary brown. Our eyes mate.
We should not be standing age to age
On this stone-littered slope in the March air,
Her fast-four to my slow-two. We should dance
The sarabande, that stately step in which
Partners do not move very close or very far apart
And yet love gaze to gaze, palm to palm.
I am her lawn ornament, her memorial tale,
The once-upon-a-time to tell her speckled does.
Neither of us stays. Neither of us goes.

Against Fear While Standing In My Woods in March

Death, tell our stories in your dancing step,
Young and tender, old as late-night's clock;
Wind and sun will hide the trail to where we wept.

You search the keep where every light is kept,
Round and round each city street and block;
Death, tell our stories in your dancing step.

Upon the ice of madness you have slipped,
To rob all time of every gentle tick and tock;
Wind and sun will hide the trail to where we wept.

I do not fear the forest paths where you have crept
To steal the barred owl in his single sleeping flock;
Death, tell our stories in your dancing step.

All will fear and then forget your claim to be adept,
The trail of poults, the huddling hen, the cock;
Wind and sun will hide the trail to where we wept.

And all our lives we went to bed then soundly slept
Despite the key you bear to every living lock.
Death, tell our stories in your dancing step.
Wind and sun will hide the trail to where we wept.

A Month before Spring, I Take Stock

I want to believe in the forsythia's winter hue,
That bee-yellow sting before the sun comes up,
Before the season's bees are even due.
Each incandescent morning's dimpled cup
Is too good to be false or even true;
No hummingbird's around to come and sup
Or separate by sight the yellow from the blue.
The wind's as frisky as a tumbling pup,
But it's too early for yellow in these brief days.
Somehow, my life is not what I had planned,
Not a season or a color I can always praise
Or pretend to. But on most days I can stand
The lemon pretense of a false sense or phrase,
Find flowers in my palm, love without demand.

Young and Beautiful

I do not want to drive off the Earth
In my Porsche Spyder, dying young
And beautiful, because I was never
Beautiful and I can barely remember
Being young, but I do recall the pushups
Of spiders by the fire on camping trips
And how their genuflection astonished
Me, creatures with no old age to come
Hurling themselves to the edge of fire.

Planting Near Highway 15

I hear the sound of plowing
Before I see it, that old sienna
Purring against all the earth.

The root-popped rows shine
Beneath the harrow's dinner plates,
A setting for eight out early

In the April air. My neighbor
Waves from the deep-worn saddle
Of a John Deere tractor's sway,

And his grin grows viral;
I catch it, take it down the road
On my trip to nowhere and back.

Every year he tears the root stitches
From his father's cornfield scars;
Every year he hugs the cropland heart.

Every year I feel the earth's old purr
As it opens wide for rain and seed,
And I come to see him drive along

The bright upturned nebula of stones
As if he were coming into land a man
Has never seen, as if he found every color

And all hues of all shades, and he stood
Up in the stirrups to sing what he has seen,
And from them, picked, to save us, green.

Today I Was Afraid Again

We know the source of light
But is the source of darkness
Only the absence of the source of light?
I keep asking where this perpetual
Uneasiness about my life
Begins or began, the fear for family
And accounts, of journeys
To lands beyond all control.
I can't say. Yearning wings in spring
Don't consider in advance the pond
That may be dried, the cricket choir
Gone silent for a solemn year.
And yet each moonbright night
For two weeks I sit up in my bed
And gasp the details of all stories'
Coming ends. Then I know again
There is no greater gift to gain
Than full knowledge and full serenity
And that I want to see them ahead,
The land I was always coming back to
In the agony of human migrations,
Not the absence of darkness
But an absence of fear in the absence
Of all light. Then I will make my peace.

The Sorrow of Mirrors

I am not reminded of David when I shave,
The boy with the sling to slug that thug Goliath
To death. I am not reminded of a lesser Pope
Slowly going to seed in the drunken palace
Of the Borgia kin. I am not reminded daily
Of Beat Generation larcenists or Ansel Adams
With his Yosemite eye on the black-and-white
World of the West. I am not reminded of monarchs
Or sun-stained farmers or Ralph Vaughn Williams
Orchestrating English folk songs because he thinks
The poor are more noble. I'm not even reminded
Of the poor Neanderthal man, diorama-bound
In the Museum of Natural History, always looking
A little befuddled by the simplest task, his big brain
Too much for anyone to carry around and use
With any facility. When I shave I'm reminded
Of the anonymity of mirrors, how they have no face
Of their own and must borrow whomever wanders
Past and for minutes be a face among no crowd,
Brilliant mimics who mistake left for right but gleam
With each new face they frame, even if it's mine.

For the Coming of Our Days
For my wife, Linda

I want to narrow it all down to one prophecy
On which I can stand, something that inevitably
Comes true or has that clear sense of prescience
Like a primary color on a cloudless autumn day.

I can't. I have tried to see with clarity into the past,
Even, and failed. I have said, At least allow me
The grace to predict a day of tactical blunders
Or the way friendship burned into fresh loving.

Today I tried to see deep into the present moment.
The ground whereon I stood by a dry fountain
Was shut down because of drought, and I wanted
To believe I smelled coming rain. But I didn't.

So tell me, how can I bring you prophecies now
Of our lives to come? We cannot even speak aloud
The weather three days on. I don't have the gift
For any future. And so I sit on our porch and fill

With fortune as the sun spills along the open sills
Of my days. I am deer and drum, child and choir,
Wheelchair lady in her warmed and shimmering spokes,
Brief days, warmed fur, the sound of your own name.

Harvesting Clothes

The best days
Of childhood for me
Came when clothes
On the line had dried
And my mother
Went out to harvest
Them in a basket.
Some were not
Quite ripe, damp
In places on the line,
And they stayed up
Unpicked, still
Stiffening with fresh
Wind. Clothespins
Clacked as she took
Them off and dropped
Them in her pocket-
Apron. I buried my
Face in the sun-fresh
Clothes, and I thought
This must be how heaven
Smells when you
Wake up there
If you died young
And had been
A good boy
All your life.

The Tides of Light

Daylight comes in tides, afternoon's ebb,
The morning full to the breakwater rocks
Of my porch. The neap of noon awakens
Suspicion that we can't tread this for long.
Late evening's two-beer backseat grapple
Of riptides almost drowns the county's kids,
Lets them up finally for air. All the day,
Light breaks and breaks up on the old shore
Of my land in blue waves, washing over
The mammary stones, lapping every root
From every tree with their rising, falling
And moon-turned heights. We bathe in them,
These strong tides with their ancestry, their
Valedictory fields of fieldstone graves.
We settle on the shores of this quiet familiarity.
We walk along the borderlines to remember
How the first swim felt in such strong light.

Offering Myself to the Woods

When I go into the green, it begins.
The hunters gather, the blades flash clean
From their legs, hawks dip down to know
If I will bear myself in time as kind prey.

Ants horse up from mound to mound.
Scorpions scuttle out to stab my step
When I have passed. The packing dogs
Howl for me in moon's cool frieze.

I am here, I say. I am the easy catch,
The sacrifice, a word for legends you tell
In ending hours. I am your meat and bread,
Your sun-grown grain. Hunt me now.

Paws come slowly toward me in the leaves.
Fins break all mirrors and rise for this bait.
Insects in their small steps and damp wings
Turn me into hymns when I go into green.

I am here. The hunters finish with me now
And in their recessional vow to speak me
New to sky and earth and water in its view
Of all this Earth. I am named. I am loved.

Rainy Day Ants

Portals sealed, all light shipped until this sky
Closes against itself: they army in warm darkness
And wait for orders from the chamber of a queen.
A thousand labyrinths hum. Workers sweat out
Their unemployment. And then stories of the flood
Begin again, of water boiling eye to eye to eye
While they learned to step from that sand boat
And walk upon it, casting miracles to follow,
Pheromones floating their ships down to sea.

Each day we may not come out again.
Each night may find us in the narrow rooms
Of our Minotaur days, lost and not quite alone,
Hearing storms' end above us, others now
Getting on with things in their natural order,
And we slower, knowing soon that what fell
Upon us was not rain, was never rain at all,
But the music of small endings, of sealing wax
And the Mason jar preservation of our days.

Making Hay

Haymaking time
Has come again
To south Oconee
And bristly pills
Fill the fields
With half a thousand
Circular meals;
And green,
And after rain,
They steam
As if to simmer
Off the season's
Sun, to smoke
Their stems
In tender lengths
While cattle wait
And hesitate
To taste the heat
And fiber knots
The evening sun's
Delight has made.

The Ruined Farmhouse Fills With Crows Who Go Silent as Rain Comes

He awakens from his death
To see it is still black
Through the windows
In the fields and in all rooms
Of his small home
But one miracle
Has come while
He has been away
And it is this:
That darkness,
That narrow night
He so feared in life
Was all along
A feast of quiet wings
And shifting skies
Weeping for the joy
Of a crop at morning time
When white wings come.

What We Carry

In bulbing time, my wife
Kneels to spade the cold soil,
In no hurry to migrate or molt
Or learn another language
Or remember how lovely
The flowers are that cling
To the iris blades in spring.

No. She holds the cool eggs
Like a turtle who covers
The perfect shells unbroken
From her body and then turns
Her back forever, knowing
That to conceive is great
But letting go is the finer act

Of love we carry with us
Always, beneath the soil
Of our bodies, where it is
Possible to flower even
When all the hope for spring
Has gone, when that first
Runner breaking from
The bulb of our deeper
Memory grows into bright life
And a sweeter scent than roses.

Table at the Four Seasons

In the restaurant of my forest
Which species serves as the waiters?
I see them in their black thorax trousers,
With mandible washcloths draped just-so,
Standing patiently to know what the others
Wish to order for their meals. Natural selection
Knows which ones can survive and serve.

They would have to remember
If the group at table four like annuals
Or perennials with their flowering nectar,
If the grubs wished deer or velvet squirrel
Just after pulpy chanterelles. In the kitchen
Of gnats and Carolina wrens, the aromas
Must be incredible to those who dine,
To those who have come here for a feast.

And the waiters, not allowed themselves
To eat the meal become the meal's
Last course and do it with a waiter's grace,
In silence and elegance, with a brief bow
And their creases taut and still in place.

Right Up to the Fence

I am a little afraid of horses.
So what? They're huge, stamp
Sonnets down the trampled paddock
While I hunt a single word; who
Wouldn't climb the fence to escape
Such facility? I want to brazen
It out, speak about fetlocks
From the corner of my mouth,
Belgians and hands-high, terms
For the others who have come
To watch. I want to fetch a plume
Of broomsedge to idly chew,
Lightly slap a ruinous rump
To show my praise. I can fool
The other men, but the horses
Have known since I got out
Of my truck. They have come
To the fence with their eyes
Like classroom globes to watch
Me, taste my fear like grain.
Their nostrils flare. Trampling
The weak is a duty to which
They are bound by all nature.
I stand aside with my single word
And let them pass, allow their
Stamping dance, this pastured storm
As they cull me from the herd.

Love Poem

Old cats forget how
To make fools of themselves
With a piece of string
Or a grocery bag
Or fingers under a cover
So if I don't make you smile
So often these days
Please understand
That I am dreaming
Of leaping right off
The safe perch of my life
With no place to land
Just to touch your hair
As you pass me
And twist impossibly
And ridiculously
Like the harmless fool
You knew in kitten days
When I was afraid
Of absolutely nothing.

Realizing Finally That Praise Will Not Come

Some water gets to be rain many times,
And some must have a single chance
To drop. This morning, a slight drizzle
Holds above the ridge and I wonder:
Is this your only chance to rise and fall?
Or did you expect storms, hail, the ecstasy
Of St. Theresa or a sailor's fearful squall?

In the quiet writing room he sits and waits
Like rain to know if he will breach the wall
And get the honors he has sought,
If his sentences can dampen cheeks,
Do anything for anyone at all.

The Great Jade Gate
Of My Estate

Might as well be jade. It might as well
Have swallow finials of sun-laid gold
And scenes from my life on a pearl frieze.
It should bear sentries in armor plate,
Each with a finely etched silver trumpet
To blast off peasants or announce to all
My departure for distant palaces or lands.
The great jade gate of my estate should
Have onyx parapets, Bose speakers,
And, and, chrome! Chrome bumpers!
And a five-speed overdrive that kicks ass
On the dirt road that runs along my land!
The great jade gate of my estate should
Actually exist to curb my redneck impulses,
To bring forth thousands to await my words
Like the writ of ages. But can't you just see
The great jade gate of my estate swing open
In its empire gloss of grandeur and out I roar
In a Chevelle 442 with two four-barrel carbs
And the radio just pounding all nations
Into submission as I pass, me in my crown,
And R&B blowing my speaker cones
Apart like the war was on and I'd already won!
Damn!

The Actor

For once, I'd prefer to fall
Not fall apart, come into the room
With my waiter's tray of drinks
For everyone and start to trip.
That's when the thrill begins,
When an accident of no special
Threat, when no one will die,
Begins to happen before our eyes.
For a moment I'd regain
My balance and keep the seven
Cocktails on the (make it) silver tray,
But bowing back, windmilling
Suddenly as if I might fly
Right out of there, a gasp
Would already be turning
Into laughter. All will say
He's falling down for no reason.
A fat pompous old man's eyes
Go wide and he gets drenched!
Love, pity, helping hands,
All for the sorrow of my stunt.
They cannot see that on this screen
I am Laurel and Balanchine.

An Injunction

Teach your children also how to grow,
To be unguarded, to show delight
At the pale duet of sun and wind
Inside a honeysuckle bloom today.

Teach them to subside. Tell them
To dig a long row for butter beans
And fill it up with costume jewelry
To see if a cabaret begins to sprout.

Teach your children that lakes
Are silver, the sky bruised yellow,
That nothing is the color we claim,
Not even a heart's old blood.

Teach your children the deep stories
Of the flood and the return home
With special instructions from owls.
Teach them to walk trailing light.

Teach your children to find tracks
Along the creek and to know which
Ones lead and which ones follow
And which ones stand still to teach.

For the End of the Last War

The world is at peace. Cattle kneel in the fields
To hear the sound from continents away.
The last shot from the last war was fired Tuesday.
Children stand to dust themselves off, stunned
To see trucks bearing food in a caravan line.

Machinery forgets its gears. Grass grows through
The cracks of the military bases and no one comes
To cut it. Cattle push the fencing down and taste
The fresh green blades that sing in the spring wind.
Heaps of weapons burn in the desert in silence.

We have lived to see this. We did not create it.
The cattle did. They watched us into waiting
With their penitential eyes. They stood on slopes
And did not own them and showed us how we
Might stand on Earth and not guard its boundaries.

The world is at peace. Men and women pour out
Of their houses into the streets. Their children
Have been there for days already. Not one lifts
His hand against another. Above the town, on hills
High enough to hear the silence, the cattle come.

Painting My Bedroom with Stars

My new bedroom was once my daughter's
And I did not know that on the walls
She had pasted glow-in-the dark stars
When she was six, two small ones close
To each other and a large one farther away.
For weeks, I closed my eyes when the light
Went out and saw nothing, but last night,
Thinking of time and distance and her eyes,
I felt troubled and lay awake in that darkness
Until I spoke her name and the stars came out.
Families let the years pass, galaxies spread
Between them, and unnamed constellations
Appear waiting for the love of a name,
For fathers and daughters to put their fingers
On the sky and claim the heavens from the dark.

Sunday Morning on the Rocks By the Creek, I Consider the End

I want to think my body is not thinking
Of giving up on me. That it has plans
To stay fit finally, hold its tone for decades
To come, as if the younger it got
The more I'd forget that I now forget
Friends' names or the day I could leap
Across a wide creek and always be dry.

I want to think my body won't let in
Anything come to kill it, that it will slay
Anaerobes in their legions, crush cancers,
And prepare me for the Olympic grandeur
Of a suspicious old age when I will be hated
Or admired equally because I would not die.

But my bones get the giggles to think of it.
My body tells my mind, Sorry, but one day
I'll close up shop and we will both be out of here.
Because I believe for me the body will go first
And that my mind will be planning picnics
On the beach with a girl a third my age

When the last day comes. I want charity
For that day, I presume, but my body shrugs.
I want to think my body is not thinking
Of letting me go mad first, but that might not
Be the worst part of this bargain, to be able
To go, even when I don't know where I'm going.

Learning to Grow Old

The shadow of a bell is another bell.
We know it well even without its ringing.
We know the moment we are out of hell
From the fading fear and then the singing.

The Edge of the Current

My beagle, Murphy, just out and fed,
Begins to scream. The howl is earthless,
Wild for felons or rustling pheasant,
Filled with full moons and moors.

What could any creature want so much
That it would cry as if original sin
Were suddenly proved beyond a doubt
To be hideously and terribly true?

Are clanking jailbirds nesting down
In the woods? Has this patch of hillslope
Gone volcanic, about to blow its cork
Like Krakatau? I wait not to know.

But my beagle cries and tells me
That it is my wife's trailing scent:
She has gone to walk at the creek
By herself. She will not be alone there

Long. Nose on the brightest scent
No one on Earth can quite catch
As she does, she's off. She's running
As if Sherlock Holmes stood to one side

Nodding and saying love finds us
Or we find love, even if we must trail it
Over and over into the deepest woods
And right to the edge of the current.

It Was All About Nothing

I love the moment
When things do not begin
To go wrong
When all I have suspected
Might happen doesn't
And I am left
Standing ankle-deep
In the amazement
Of relief
And do not even bother
To reconstruct
The time that I lost
Worrying about
What did not happen
Or feel shame
That I could have
Been looking forward
To this quiet joy
That is almost like
An ache, the kind
That reminds us
To get on home
Where nothing bad
Will happen
For the rest
Of all time.

Words for the City Poets

You poets of gritty urban realism,
You poets of curb sludge and Bukowski bars,
You poets of apartments & ampersands,
You poets of lower-case first-person pronouns,
You poets of irony and cigarettes,
You poets of blind alleys and fire escapes,
You poets where poetry must be slammed,
You poets of savagery and its victories:

I give you the madness of whippoorwills,
I give you the intoxication of deciduous wind,
I give you the flicker's pine-tree hutch,
I give you the smoke of mist at dawn,
I give you the blindness of moondark pastures,
I give you the bloody calf against the cow in snow,
I give you the creek and the river, cuts in earth,
I give you what the country knows.

Parable of the Carpenter Bee

I tell my daughter not to worry,
It's just a carpenter bee,
And she asks: What does it build, then,
If it's a carpenter? I show her
How it drills holes in our porch,
Leaving conical piles of dust,
How it hums while it works
As if it has lost all the words.
She says, It's just tearing up
The porch; it's not building
Anything, is it? So why call
It a carpenter bee is what I want
To know. Every living thing
Builds or has built for it a space
In which to live, but we don't call
Them carpenter anything, do we?

Sometimes we don't see what's built
Or even what we build ourselves
For years. We nail one word to another
And one day there's a shed for tools,
And two children later it's a bungalow
With three bedrooms and a modest view.
We dig for no special reason, hoping
That a special reason will present itself
Along the way, that someone will say,
I admire what you have built for yourself
Here, and for a moment we don't quite know
What he's talking about, and then we see
The sawdust from our lives and turn
Sharply to see what it was we made
For all those years with our digging hands.   ➢

But most of the time we're going
Nowhere special, just humming
As we drill, hoping to understand
Why we have come here to hide
And that it makes us safe from nothing
In the end, that it's just a gentle lie,
For carpenters also build, then die.

Diplomacy

A family with two pit bulls has moved in
Next door, and when the dogs are loose
And wander over and I shoo them home,
They look so hurt and bewildered that I
Almost want to apologize. Their stump tails
Dig down to wag deep greetings, but I am
Resolute in not wanting them around, so I
Clap my hands and shout, as if a prayer meeting
Had broken out, as if there were an all-day
Dinner on the grounds and they were not welcome.

They run forty yards into the woods and stop
And turn to me with sad eyes as if to say
What of Buchenwald and Sand Creek? Explain
How Dresden turned to flames and the feral
Glint of child killers loose in the tame world
Of your imaginary order. Why would you
Believe us less to walk your lovely land?

Some day, I tell them with my eyes, we will
Know each other better, perhaps, but now,
Here, in the distance of necessary outposts
And all the weakness bred in all our bones,
We stay apart. We will cry to each other again
And one day soon the fence will fall apart
And I will bark you to the edge of my yard
Where you can taste these bones and understand
My strength and my weakness. We will forgive.
But for now I am afraid of what you may not
Even know or remember or what I may not
Even know or remember, and how we are bound
To it by something worse than all our blood.

Cat in the Piano

The Bach I played went bad, as if its sell-by date
Had passed. The treble run turned plinky, tin,
And knowing that I owned a Grand and that
Its purchased sound should shine ripe as apples
Almost due to fall, I played the right-hand run again.
The sound was worse, quite tubby, even fat,
And so I stood to see the demon in the strings
But only saw, amazed to watch the hammers strike,
And lying there to catch that mouse, our cat.

He strummed the notes and cocked his head,
Gently pawed the hammer, wanting that rise and fall
To start again. He purred, mad for small bourées,
And let his eyes dance string to string to see
If music might come back by wishing it along.
I thought how Bach would love this rumble
Since in those days to lie among the spring of notes
And live long did not occur as often as a lovely note,
So I played and the cat played, and the counterpoint
Was what we miss most in this unplayful world,
The song that goes with ours that we never hear,
The good days we weave without even knowing it.

Early Morning, Autumn

I just want to be quiet
Now, I just want to lie
On a slab of memory

In the river and feel it
Wash around me, but
Not actually hear the water,

Just feel it, the way skin
Felt on an apple in the fall
When I wiped on a shine

With my hands and thought
I had created something
More beautiful than belief.

I just want to be silent
And mean anything,
The color red, foam,

Water kicking up its heels
Before evaporating
In the last waterfall before the coast.

A Message for You

Remind me to visit
The dying but do not
Remind me to die.

Remind me to light
The lilies with water
If rain does not come.

But do not remind me
To bind them stem
To stem for wreaths.

Remind me to suffer
If suffering is due
And no one else comes

To take the job. I will
Be glad for your visit
As I do not shout aloud.

Remind me to live,
So few do it for long
That when we see

A girl lit up, bright
As an incandescent coil,
We glow along, too.

Remind me to check
The Periodic Table
Of the Elements to see

If love has made it
After oxygen and no one
Has noticed, not even

The great scientists
Who claim to know
Why the dying need

Visitors but have not
Yet visited themselves.
Which is why I will come

Straight with lilies
And a bright-eyed girl
To the bedside rites

Of the suffering. We
Will bring water
And sweet permission

For surrender and say
We are here because
You asked us to come,

Because in your sorrow
You sought us out
And healed our hearts.

ABOUT THE AUTHOR

Philip Lee Williams is the author of 13 books and the winner of numerous awards and honors for his work, including the Michael Shaara Award for his 2004 Civil War novel *A Distant Flame*. He is a winner of the Townsend Prize for fiction and has twice been named Georgia Author of the Year. His books have been translated into a number of languages, and in 2007, he was named winner of a Georgia Governor's Award in the Humanities. His poetry has been published in more than forty magazines, including, *Poetry, Karamu,* the *Kentucky Poetry Review,* and *Press*. He has taught creative writing at the University of Georgia and given lectures and readings of his work for the past 25 years. For eighteen years, he and his family have lived in the woods on a dirt road in Oconee County in north central Georgia. The poetry in this volume is centered on that rural area and on Wildcat Creek, which borders their land.